OFFICIAL
FORTNITE
THE CHRONICLE VOL. 2

CONTENTS

JUMP TO IT!

Fortnite's multi-year journey has been a nonstop thrill ride. So much has happened since Fortnite first launched that even the most invested fans probably missed something along the way.

That's where this book comes in. It recaps all the major events, surprises, and changes so far, allowing you to get up to speed. It starts right at the beginning and goes all the way to Chapter 2: Season 2.

Whether you're here to reflect on your own experiences of Battle Royale or to fill a few blank spots in your knowledge of the game's evolution, enjoy taking this journey back in time. There's a lot to cover, so let's get started. To the Battle Bus!

WELCOME TO THE WORLD OF

FORTNITE

CLIMB ABOARD THE BATTLE BUS AND GET READY TO SHOW OFF YOUR SKILLS

Fortnite is a modern-day phenomenon, with millions of players having discovered the thrill of a Battle Royale, and huge numbers returning to the island on a regular basis. There are all kinds of factors that have helped it become one of the most popular games on the planet, so let's round up some of the most important ones....

AN EVER-EVOLVING EXPERIENCE

Whether you've been away from the game for a month, a week, or even just a day, there's always something new to see or do every time you log in. From regular Item Shop updates where you might find your new favorite Outfit, to Limited Time Modes and events that are only around for a short while, it's worth checking in as often as you can in case you miss out on something exciting!

SOMETHING FOR EVERYONE

Want to play solo and take on the world? Go for it—just remember to watch your back, because nobody else will do it for you! Want to team up with others and enjoy safety in numbers? Good thinking, and there are modes that can cater to groups of up to four. Looking for a larger brawl? Check out large team modes that let you engage in massive battles! However you like to play, the game always has you covered.

EXPRESS YOURSELF

With hundreds of unique items available for each of the various slots in the Locker, it's super easy to create a look that sets you apart from everyone else that drops in. Show off your old-school credentials with an Outfit from an early season, mix and match to create an awesome getup, or just use whatever combination of stuff you think looks cool.

PLAY WITH ANYONE, ANYWHERE

Cross-platform support lets you team up with your friends no matter what platform they play Fortnite on, so there are no limits when it comes to getting your squad together! The in-game "ping" system even lets you mark up useful items or highlight enemies without the need for voice communication.

NO TWO GAMES ARE THE SAME

Sometimes you'll luck into a few chests full of amazing gear within seconds of touching down, but other games you'll have to test your skills with a couple of Common weapons. Maybe sometimes you'll want to run a shotgun, but others you'll grab an SMG instead. Where you drop can also make a huge difference to what kind of game you get.

THE STORY SO FAR

FORTNITE'S FIRST NINE SEASONS LAID THE FOUNDATIONS FOR THE CURRENT GAME

This is where it all began. In July 2017, something happened that changed the gaming landscape forever: Fortnite arrived. A few months later, in September, it added a 100-player Battle Royale mode. The game's fast-paced, ever-changing action proved to be an instant hit with players worldwide. Over 10 million people dropped from the Battle Bus in the first two weeks after the game's release.

Over the following four years Fortnite kept growing. A constantly evolving landscape, thrilling plot twists, a vast array of outlandish Outfits, and quirky weapons meant that there was always something exciting happening.

Join us now as we take a look back at where it all began, in the early seasons of what we now know was Fortnite Chapter 1....

This first season was the only one not to have a Battle Pass as we know it today. Leveling up granted access to a handful of exclusive cosmetics, which now serve as badges of honor—if you have any of those Outfits, players are going to know you've got years of experience!

Season 2 introduced the Battle Pass, with 70 tiers of rewards to unlock. This provided a great incentive for players to keep jumping back in search of those exclusive rewards. This season's Battle Pass was themed around knights and chivalry, with three unique medieval Outfits to unlock.

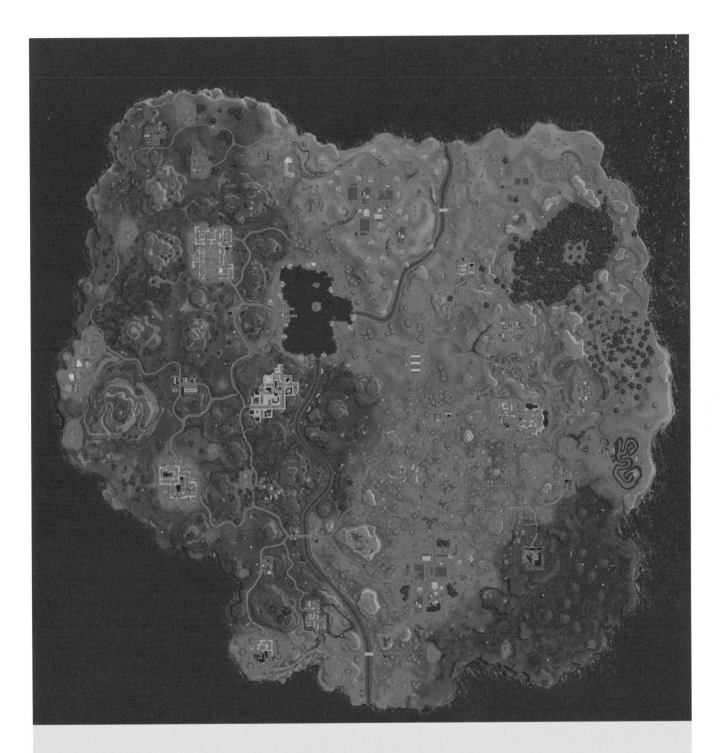

SEASON 1 AND 2

The island, when we first visited it back in Season 1, was a lush, green paradise, though there were some built-up areas, including Greasy Grove and Retail Row. As the game moved into Season 2, however, the greenery receded in a couple of places, and several favorite Fortnite locations appeared for the very first time, including Tilted Towers, Snobby Shores, and Lucky Landing. Players would come to know and love these locations.

In Season 3, Fortnite looked to the stars with a space theme. The Battle Pass was expanded to now offer 100 tiers of rewards to players. It was also the season that an underlying narrative started to emerge within the game, with eagle-eyed players spotting a meteor in the sky and theorizing that it could come crashing down onto the island. They were proven right when a comet struck Tilted Towers. As the season came to a close, a larger meteor laid waste to Dusty Depot. This kind of game-changing development has come to be par for the course with Fortnite now, and each new season is ushered in by a major event that sets up a very different experience.

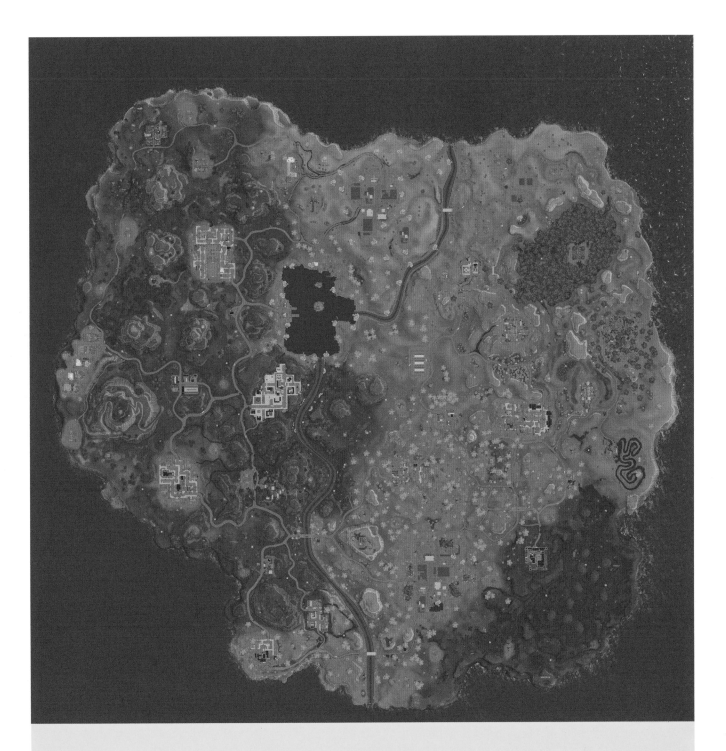

SEASON 3

At first, the Season 3 map seemed reassuringly familiar—if increasingly crowded, as more and more new players started hopping on the Battle Bus! But then people spotted a meteor in the sky, headed toward the island. Over the course of the season, it got closer and closer before smashing into Dusty Depot, leaving Dusty Divot in its wake. A research facility was put in place to analyze the meteor, setting up what was to come in Season 4.

Season 4 saw Fortnite go to the movies, with a cinema and superhero theme. The meteor impact that signaled the transition between seasons continued to alter the game, first spawning items called Hop Rocks before events spiraled toward chaos. It wasn't just a meteor, you see—the giant space rock also contained an alien pod containing The Visitor, who used the Hop Rocks to turn a movie rocket into a real one. Millions of players gathered to see the rocket take flight.

Things started to get strange on the island in Season 5, with the rifts left by the rocket wreaking havoc on the weather while

allowing players a new way to get around the map. These weren't the only thing to aid mobility, either, with the ATK vehicle able to carry an entire squad to remote locations quickly. The rifts had one last trick up their sleeves: They spawned a cube that hovered across the map, settling at Loot Lake, where it changed the location.

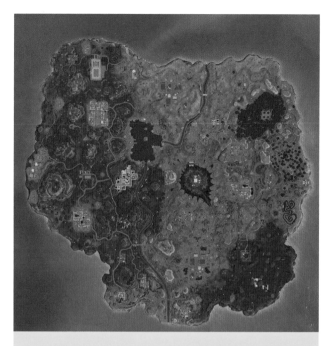

SEASON 4

A research facility was built in Wailing Woods as scientists began examining the crashed meteor. Meanwhile, a villain lair appeared in Snobby Shores, leading to the creation of a rocket.

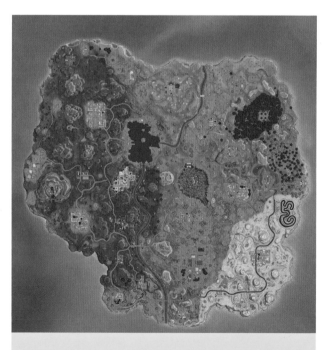

SEASON 5

With the rifts created by the rocket altering the map, things started to look a little sunnier. Moisty Mire was replaced by Paradise Palms. The island even got its own golf resort.

In Season 6 the runes left by the cube began to corrupt the areas around them, creating Shadow Stones that transformed their users into wisp-like entities with greatly increased agility. Soon, the freshly re-formed cube started revisiting all of these rune locations, absorbing power from each in turn before returning to the lake for the next step of its plan. Now it started to spew out Cube Monsters, AI enemies that could be killed for loot. The cube later crumbled and exploded, yet the location was recreated by a mysterious force. Late in the season, players began to notice an iceberg drifting toward the island. Things were about to get very chilly....

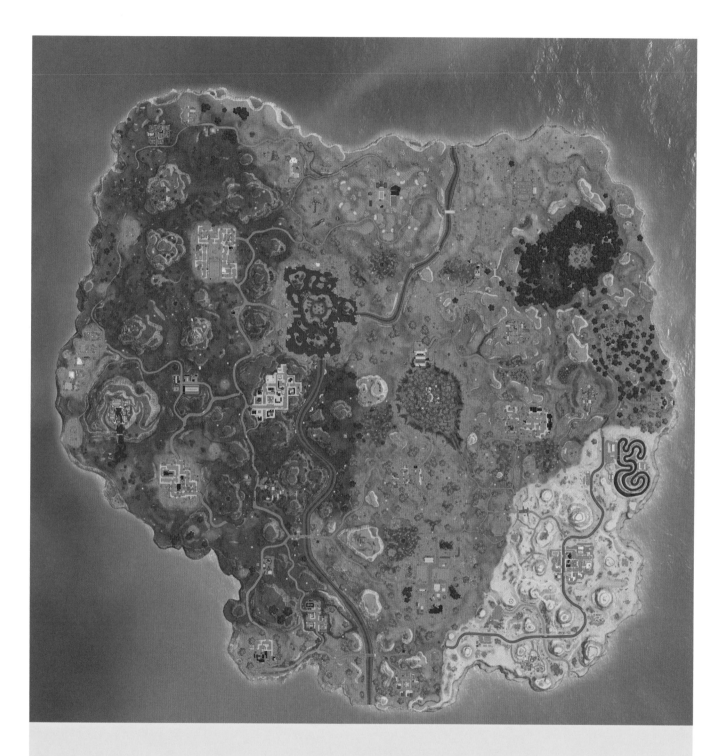

SEASON 6

At this point, the island map was being updated weekly, meaning there was always something new to see. At the start of the season, Loot Lake was corrupted, with the water initially turning purple before a giant whirlpool formed. A suitably spooky castle appeared in Haunted Hills overlooking the graveyard, while the buildings at Wailing Woods expanded, including a shack with a secret underground bunker.

Season 7 took Fortnite to new heights, with an ice-coated mountain and the addition of the game's first aerial vehicle, the X-4 Stormwing. As it turns out, the iceberg that collided with the island was actually the lair of a new villain, the Ice King, who emerged late in the season to spread monsters known as Ice Fiends onto the map.

Defeating these creatures only complicated matters, however. An evil prisoner escaped from the castle, fleeing to Wailing Woods before finally causing a volcano to emerge.

Pirates arrived in Season 8, setting up camps all over the map. The northeast corner was a brand-new place to explore,

with the volcano, the newly formed Lazy Lagoon, and Sunny Steps offering new loot hotspots. In addition, lava pools popped up around the volcano, allowing players to ride the hot-air currents. The government intervened, setting up excavation sites, one of which contained a bunker for survivors to hunker down in.

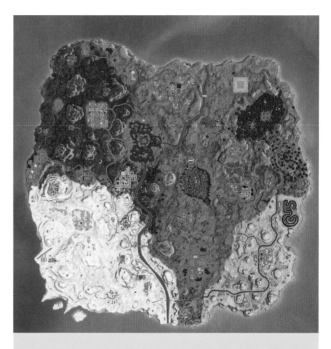

SEASON 7

As the iceberg smashed into the island, the temperature dropped and the southwest corner became covered in snow. A new land mass also emerged, extending the map further.

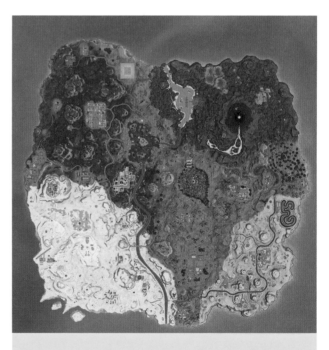

SEASON 8

While the pirates built their forts, a jungle grew up around a volcano, which erupted spewing lava to the south. Some large wooden animals also appeared dotted around the island.

What players saw when they emerged in Season 9 would blow their minds. While the survivors were holed up, the entire island had been completely rebuilt. Tilted Towers was reborn as Neo Tilted, with high-tech buildings and travel tubes. Grav-lifts carried thrill-seekers to platforms which made excellent loot sniper nests. The icecaps still had a surprise in store, with the volcanic activity allowing a monster to escape. To combat it, work began on constructing a giant mech. What followed was an epic clash between machine and beast, with the mech emerging victorious and saving the island for the final season in this chapter of Fortnite....

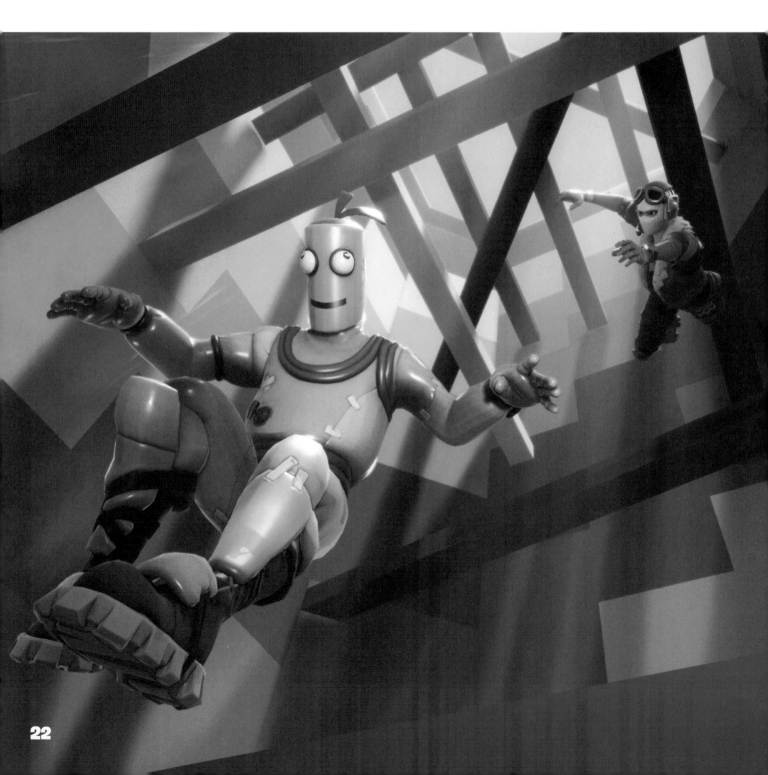

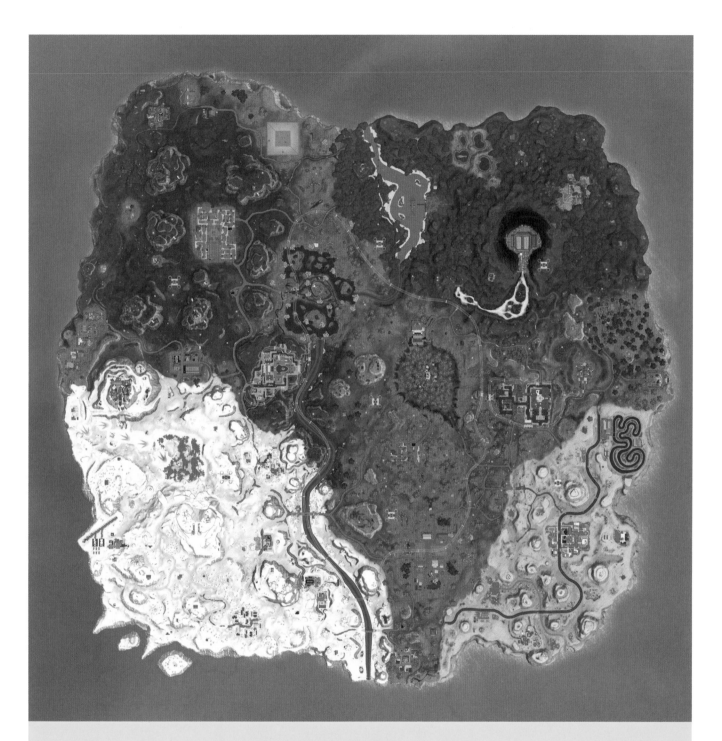

SEASON 9

With the pirates having abandoned the island, the mega corporations took over and rebuilt it as a high-tech paradise instead. Tilted Towers became Neo Tilted, and Retail Row was replaced with Mega Mall. The volcano, now completely dormant, was transformed into a power station called Pressure Plant, while the slipstream turbines allowed you to move around the map quickly. Even Loot Lake underwent a futuristic makeover.

CHAPTER 1:
SEASON X

WELCOME TO THE END OF THE WORLD

All good things must come to an end, including the first chapter of Fortnite. Season X used the theme of time to bring back all manner of things from the game's past, including numerous locations and weapons.

The Visitor returned, but this time he was able to use the facilities at Dusty Depot to start work on another rocket. If it seemed like history repeating, that's because it was, and the meteor, too, could be seen moving gradually closer to its original impact zone.

As the season came to a close, rockets, meteors, rifts, and other anomalies peppered the skies. The chaos created a black hole that sucked up the island, its residents, and in a development that shocked the world, the entire game!

GAME CHANGERS
SENDING CHAPTER 1 OFF IN STYLE

B.R.U.T.E. FORCE

Season X sure delivered some heavy hardware. The B.R.U.T.E. mech suit is a two-person vehicle with some amazing capabilities for both offensive and defensive action.

ALTERED LOCATIONS

The rifts disappeared, but their effects lingered. Some rift-tainted areas on the map would now disable building; others messed with gravity...It meant you had to really think on your feet.

OPENING A RIFT

The Junk Rift called upon the power of the gateways. The exact item that would drop was random, but the falling debris could devastate structures.

LIKE COMING HOME

Season X brought back a few famous landmarks. Dusty Depot, Retail Row, and Greasy Grove all returned to the map for a fun little blast of nostalgia.

LONG-RANGE SUPPRESSION

Sniper rifles tend to trade away fire rate for impact, but this weapon offered a new way to tackle enemies with steady streams of accurate shots.

MAP WATCH

TIME AND TIME AGAIN

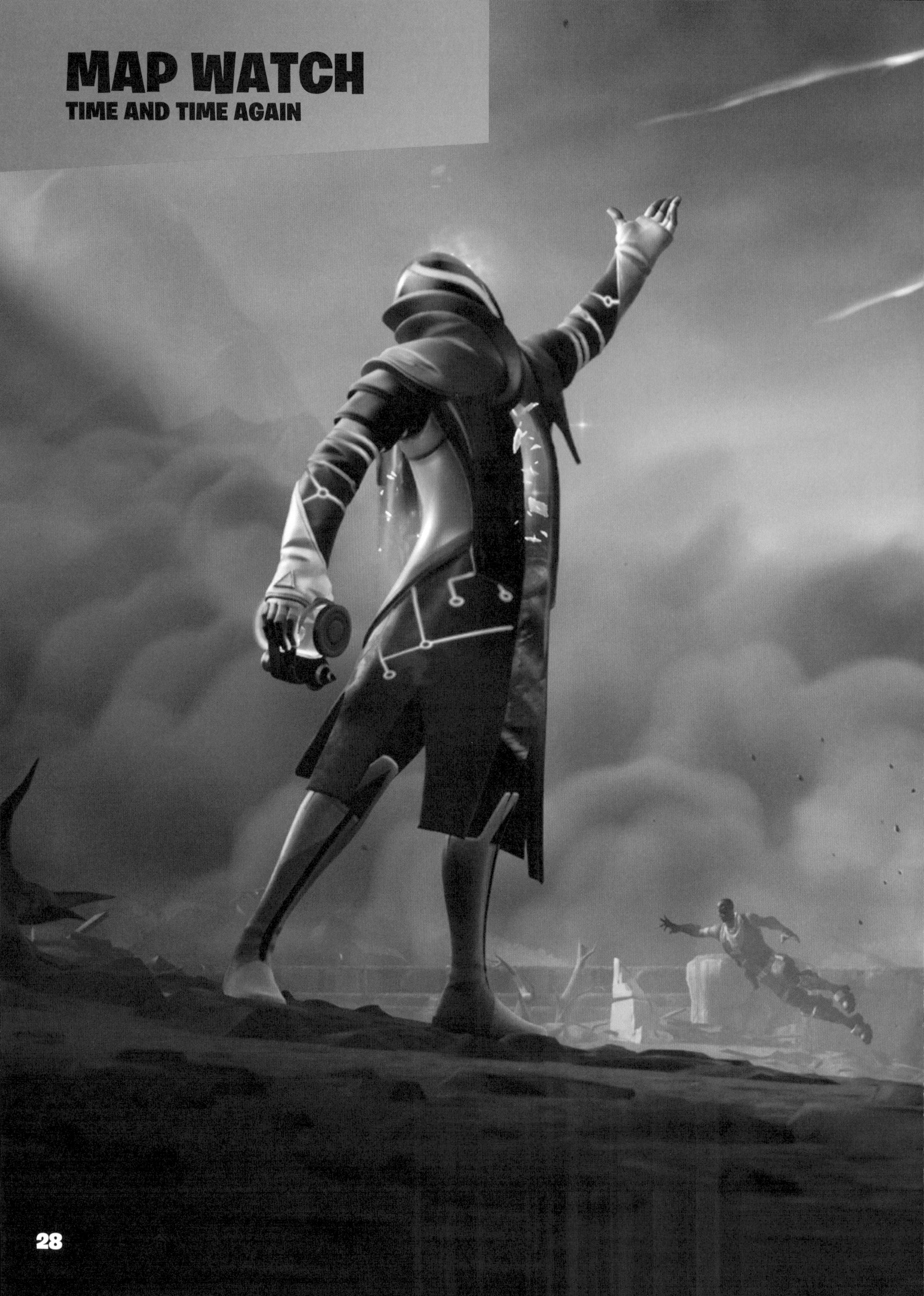

WORTH THE RISK?

The glitched consumables you encountered could turn into literally any item from the past nine seasons, making them a risky but sometimes extremely lucrative pickup!

HISTORY REPEATING

Season X's underlying theme offered Fortnite an opportunity to look back. You could use Vaulted gear to trash enemies in new locations. Missed the meteor? It's back. Never got to see the cube? Step right up. Season X's map was a Greatest Hits of Fortnite's locations.

LOCKER LOOT
FORTNITE'S GREATEST HITS, REVISITED

OUTFITS REINVENTED

With the season's theme, the Battle Pass Outfits riffed on styles from the past. Tier 1 would get you Catalyst and X-Lord, the female counterpart of Drift and an alternate-universe Rust Lord respectively. Teknique got an update in the form of Tilted Teknique. The last two took us back to Season 2—Sparkle Supreme filled in for Sparkle Specialist, while Black Knight was reborn as Ultima Knight.

30

ESSENTIAL EXTRAS

KITSUNE

Who in their right mind would say no to having a Drift-themed fox pup Pet? This was a low-tier Battle Pass reward.

STEELWING

Make a monstrous entrance on a huge metallic dragon that flies you into battle...Do we need to say more?

KEVIN

A purple runic wrap that takes its name from the nickname for the strange cube that roamed the map.

SPARKLE SCYTHE

The neon blade and angular body of this are just stunning, and it feels as good as it looks.

MISSION UPDATE
CHALLENGES GET MORE CHALLENGING

A NEW SYSTEM

Season X introduced the Mission system, with each mission taking the form of a to-do list of tasks that would expand as players checked off each one. These ensured that there was always something to work toward. Checking off every task didn't just end the Mission—it leveled it up.

WORK TOGETHER

Struggling with a challenge? You could use your Party Assist to help by having friends' activity count toward objectives, so you would rarely get truly stuck.

33

MEMORABLE MOMENTS

THE KEY EVENTS THAT CHANGED THE WORLD OF FORTNITE FOREVER

THE MISSILE

The launch of the rocket in Season 4 was Fortnite's first real event. It crashed into Tilted Towers and opened a rift, before tearing a hole in the sky.

THE CUBE

This mystery played out over several seasons. After a tour of the island, the cube ended up at Loot Lake and eventually drew players into an alternate dimension.

THE METEOR

Players wondered whether this was more than just a visual effect. They had an answer when the rock leveled Dusty Divot at the end of the season!

THE FINAL SHOWDOWN

When a monster was let loose on the island, construction began on a gigantic mech suit. It led to an epic battle, but the creature was finally defeated. Phew!

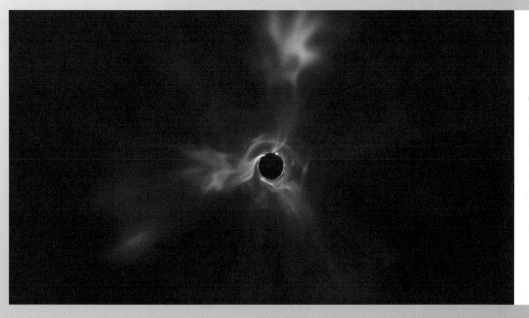

THE END

By the end of Season X, the island had seen its fair share of disasters, but nobody was ready for the game itself to be sucked into a black hole!

THE 2019 FORTNITE WORLD CUP

A LOOK BACK AT THE FIRST YEAR OF THE HIGH-STAKES GAMING EVENT

July 2019 saw Fortnite fever reach a new high, with the inaugural Fortnite World Cup finals taking place at the Arthur Ashe tennis stadium in Queens, New York.

An incredible 40 million players entered the open qualifiers, which were eventually whittled down to just 50 teams of two in the duos event, and 100 solo players. It's no surprise that the event was so popular—there was some $30 million up for grabs as prize money!

It was popular with onlookers, too, with over 27,000 people attending the event in person and over 2 million watching the stream online. Here are some of the top results....

THE PRO-AM TOURNAMENT

The finals kicked off with the Pro-Am tournament: a coming-together of 50 pro players and 50 celebrities in a duos match, which included the likes of **Marshmello**, **Ninja**, **RL Grime**, **Tfue**, **RJ Mitte**, and many more huge names.

A massive $3 million was up for grabs to go to charity, and after five intense matches, including **Ninja** and **Marshmello** fighting to defend their throne after last year's Pro-Am, **Airwaks** and **RL Grime** emerged victorious overall, despite not earning a single Victory Royale! The points system meant their consistently high placements earned them $1 million for charity, followed by **SinOoh** and **Oking** in second, and **Jelty** and **Gaborever** in third.

CREATIVE FINALS

In the Creative Finals, eight teams of players, including Creative mode experts and big names like **Ninja** and **Cizzorz**, fought it out on a bunch of custom maps for another $3 million prize pool. **Fish Fam** swam to victory, which meant that **Cizzorz**, **Tyler**, **Zand**, and **Suezhoo** shared over $1.3 million between them.

DUOS FINALS

For the main event, the Duos Finals was up first; five matches on the Season 9 island. Heavy hitters were here, including **Kinstaar** and **Hunter** from Solary, **ZexRow** and **Vinny1x** from TSM, and **Elevate** and **Ceice** from 100 Thieves.

Eventually though, the Austrian and Norwegian pair of **Aqua** and **Nyhrox** came out on top, two relatively unknown players at the time who shot to stardom and became the first ever Fortnite World Champions—proving that it really is talent that matters.

SOLOS FINALS

The Solo Finals closed out the Fortnite World Cup. This was the big deal—100 players who had proven themselves to be the best in the world went head-to-head, including **Tfue**, **Mongraal**, and **Funk**, and many unknowns.

Bugha took the first match in dominant fashion with nine eliminations and managed to hold onto his overall lead in the second match by a single point, while **Skite** was the sole survivor. His two eliminations only pushed him up to sixth, though, while **Commandment**, a 14-year-old player from TSM, shot up to third. **King** was another player all eyes were on as he racked up a total of twelve eliminations across the two matches. He was eliminated at the start of the third game, however, so he had to wait to try and knock **Bugha** off the top spot.

Game four went by and despite not winning, **Bugha**'s consistent performances meant that he retained the lead. All he had to do was keep placing consistently and surviving till the endgame. In game five he did just that with a top-five finish. **Bugha** once again soared in the final match with five eliminations and a fifth-placed finish, which meant he took the lead and stayed there. A whopping 59 points, 26 above **Psalm** in second, meant that he walked away with $3 million at just sixteen. **EpikWhale**, **Kreo**, and **King** rounded out the top five.

$3 MILLION

Kyle "Bugha" Biersdorf was the first ever Fortnite Solo World Champion and won $3 million at just sixteen years old.

THE END

At the end of Season X, the rocket by Dusty Depot launched once more, as it had in Season 4. This time, however, it activated a bunch of other rifts in the sky. Eventually, one of these appeared below the meteor that had been hanging above the factories all season long. The meteor then entered the rift. Clearly, something big was afoot...

That "something big" was a huge rift that opened up, followed by a red laser aimed at the center of Loot Lake. The rockets and meteor followed it and, when the meteor struck the island, all players present were shot into the sky and sucked into the ensuing black hole.

For the next few days, anyone booting up Fortnite was greeted by the sight of the black hole in the far distance, emitting a dim blue light.

As time went on, numbers started to appear around the black hole—11, 146, 2, 36, 160, and so on. But the game itself seemed to be gone. This was unprecedented. Players had no idea what was happening!

Fans quickly figured out the significance of those numbers: If you matched each of these to the respective word in the Visitor's Season X Out of

Time challenge recordings, it read: "I was not alone, others are outside the loop, this was not calculated, The Nothing is now inevitable."

Rumors started to circulate that this could genuinely be the end of Fortnite. The event broke viewership records on both Twitter and Twitch, and it was one of the most-watched YouTube gaming events of all time. For the two

days that Fortnite would eventually hover in tantalizing darkness, Epic Games remained silent, only increasing the anticipation and fevered speculation among players and the media.

Of course, as we know now, Fortnite hadn't gone for good. The end of this first phase was merely the beginning of something much larger and more exciting. When it returned, Fortnite

Chapter 2 had begun with a complete refresh. After over two years of memorable battles, players got to stretch their legs on a brand-new island map.

New weapons, Outfits, items, vehicles, even new mechanics like carrying downed players were introduced. Now we're well into the new chapter and the game is bigger and better than ever.

CHAPTER 2:
SEASON 1

FROM THE DARKNESS, FORTNITE IS BORN ANEW

Players had been waiting for days, staring at nothing but a black hole. Then, suddenly, the game sprang back into life. A brand-new map, changes to the weapons and items, a reworked progression system....Chapter 2 opened with a bang as players dropped in for the first time.

Much of the map started out shrouded in mystery, and players would have to explore to reveal the locations and landmarks and mark them on the map for future visits. The map has more water than before, so all of the old vehicles were consigned to the Vault to make way for the Motorboat. Swimming was also improved, and there were even a series of time trials to help players hone their skills. And since you can now use weapons while swimming, getting wet can actually be a viable strategy for play.

GAME CHANGERS
NEW CHAPTER, NEW EXPERIENCES

A WHOLE NEW WORLD

The brand-new map combines the best elements of the original with a bunch of cool new places to discover. Landmarks litter the map and can be great places to gear up away from all the early action.

MESSING AROUND ON THE RIVER

All of the old vehicles got tossed into the Vault, to be replaced by a Motorboat. Packing long-range missiles that can lay waste to structures with ease, it has room on board for a full squad.

LIMIT BREAK

This chapter made leveling up an endless ride. While rewards still cap out after 100 tiers, you can now earn experience way beyond that old limit.

GO FISH

The Fishing Rod is very useful. Some of the fish that can be reeled in serve as healing items, and it's even possible to "catch" items and weapons—even a hard-to-find Mythic Goldfish.

HOSTILE TAKEOVER

Mysterious organization E.G.O. has set up outposts around the island, ranging from checkpoints to sprawling complexes. The barracks is a great place to gear up.

MAP WATCH
EXPLORE A BRAND-NEW ISLAND

FOG OF WAR

Chapter 2 did away with the original map and exploring an all-new landscape was a big part of finding your footing in the new season. None of the key locations were marked at first, requiring players to discover landmarks themselves before they'd be revealed on the map.

REVEAL YOUR DARK SIDE

This season's Battle Pass offered a new gimmick. The Outfits all came in their hero form, but completing challenges would allow you to unlock alter egos. Remedy, for example, rocks a wholesome medic look but morphs into green-haired health hazard Toxin. Turk vs Riptide changes from fisherman to pirate. Then there's Rippley, who goes all red and nasty when you unlock his alter ego, Sludge.

ESSENTIAL EXTRAS

DOWNPOUR

Scoring a Victory Royale could net you this umbrella made of the very thing it's designed to protect you from.

MONKS

An adorable and eye-catching sock monkey Outfit, what's not to like? If in doubt, send in the monkey!

SLUDGEHAMMER

Rippley's weapon changes while equipped, appearing as a mallet one moment, then a blade the next.

HIGHLIGHT STRIKERS

Cameo's neon blades are as flashy as she is, and they're one of the more striking pickaxe options.

LOCATION, LOCATION
EXPLORING THE NEW MAP

SWEATY SANDS

This resort looks out over a cove in the northwest corner of the map. Hit the pier if you're looking to gear up, or kick back and do some fishing. The small islands near the lagoon all hide secrets of their own, too.

SLURPY SWAMP

Brave the bogs in the southwest and you'll find the Slurp factory. The liquid flows out into the surrounding rivers and marshes, allowing you to slowly top up your Shields by staying in the Slurpy water for a while.

FRENZY FARM

This has everything you could want: Barns and farmhouses contain chests loaded with loot, while haystacks and fields make natural hiding spots.

LAZY LAKE

A lakeside settlement that is a fair way inland. The urban sprawl offers plenty of gear, and the surrounding waterways make for great escape routes.

WEEPING WOODS

North of Slurpy Swamp lies this forest, which offers natural cover for sneakier players. Shacks and lodges can also be great places to hole up.

SEARCH AND DESTROY
BOMB SQUAD, REPORTING FOR DUTY

A NEW WAY TO PLAY

As Chapter 2's first season drew to a close, a new mode was featured. Search and Destroy has been around as a Creative Mode for a while, but this was its time to share the spotlight with all of the mainstay modes.

BOMBS AWAY

The objective is simple, but not easy—two teams of six players face off against one another on custom maps, with the attackers looking to plant and defend bombs at the key sites while the defenders must prevent them from doing so. Chaos ensues!

SWITCHING SIDES

The game plays out over multiple rounds, with teams swapping sides to each have a go at the two different roles. Perform well and you'll earn coins, which can be used to pick up new gear at the start of each round. Alternatively, felled foes drop weapons.

A OR B?

While each map has two bomb sites (labeled A and B), only one bomb can be planted in each round. Keep defenders guessing by mixing up which you attack and how you approach, or seek out vantage points that let you see where the enemy team might be headed.

CHAPTER 2:
SEASON 2

WORTH ITS WEIGHT IN GOLD

The second season certainly had its fair share of surprises up its sleeves. The map itself remained more or less the same, save for the addition of a handful of hideouts—new locations where AI guards are always on the lookout for intruders, making it possible to be knocked out of the game before you even encountered another player. These new loot hot spots changed how people played the game, each of them offering huge amounts of gear (including unique weapons) that would attract players at the start of any given match. Competition was fierce to get your hands on those Mythic-tier boss weapons, though.

This season also brought a PvE aspect to Battle Royale in a more meaningful manner, and forced players to fight over special weapons that only one player per game could grab.

GAME CHANGERS
FACTIONS GET IN ON THE ACTION

MARAUDING MINIONS

The new landmarks offered loot, but they were heavily guarded. AI goons would patrol and they didn't pull any punches—rolling up without gearing up first was a surefire way to get booted out of the game early.

SPILL THE BEANS

The Shakedown option was added to downed enemies in order to flag up chests and enemies in the nearby area. But it could also be used on rival players in team modes, revealing the locations of nearby allies.

UNVAULTED!

The new landmarks brought their own surprises. Weapons that were Vaulted could be found, along with the unique weapons used by the hideout bosses.

THE DOCTOR IS IN

A simple change to consumables allowed players with healing items to share them with their teammates. Toss equipped heals to the ground with a button press.

SPY GAMES

This season's unique mode allowed players to side with either the Shadow or Ghost organizations, then jump into objective-based team modes.

THE RIG

Another offshore opportunity to load up on loot, but this oil platform could be tricky to find your way around if you weren't familiar with the layout. It was always worth a visit for a chance to grab TNTina's bow—a twist on the classic Boom Bow that came with regenerating ammo.

ENTER THE GROTTO

Located between Dirty Docks and Retail Row is an underground base of the kind favored by supervillains. Watch out for the AI guards and Brutus with his Minigun.

STYLISH SPIES

This season's Battle Pass granted access to a host of special agents. Bouncer Brutus had black and white variants. Tier 60 reward Meowscles has to be one of the most brilliant and bizarre Outfits to date, sporting a ripped torso with a cat head. And Tier 100 Outfit Midas brought a touch of bling with his solid-gold physique.

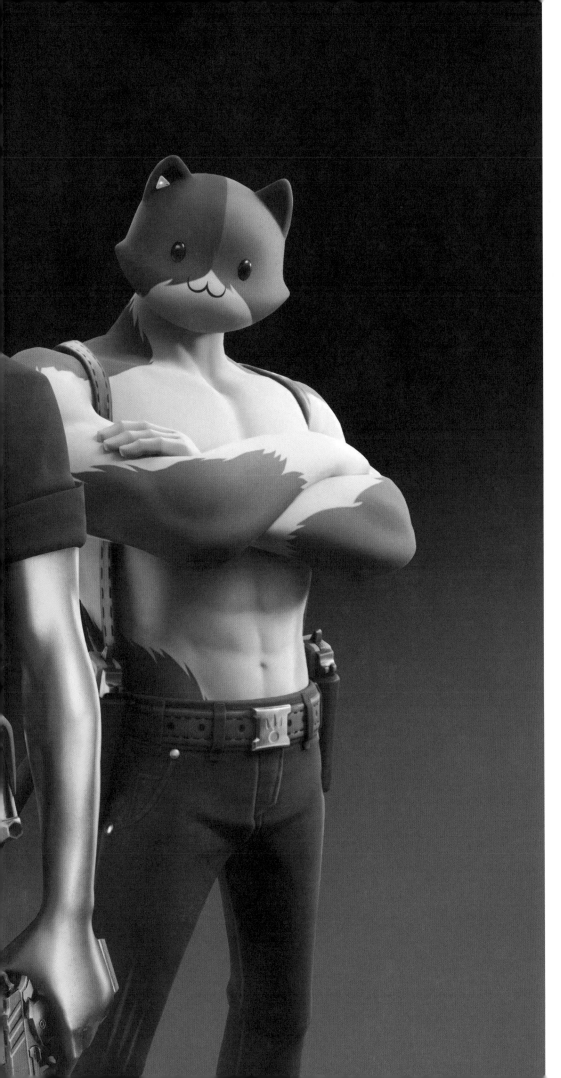

BIG HAUL

Make it rain with this glider, but cross your fingers that opponents don't try to follow the money.

EPIC SWORDS OF WONDER

Swap out your usual harvesting tool for a pair of fancy swords and live out your best fantasy life.

BOMBS AWAY!

The first ride-on Glider lets you surf on your missile (rather than hanging off it) all the way to the ground. Boom!

PANDEMONIUM

Need a distraction? Look no farther than this Emote. You can even move around while smacking your pans!

SPY GAMES
MORE OF THE THINGS THAT MADE THIS SEASON

MEET MAYA
Completing Challenges allowed you to select various parts for Maya, a fully customizable character. There were so many different options that there could be more than a million different Mayas out there!

MAP IT OUT
The Challenge Table enabled players to pinpoint where Challenges and objectives were prior to jumping in. These were flagged up with on-screen prompts when you entered an area that had uncompleted Challenge goals.

IT'S JUST A BOX...

Never underestimate the stealth potential of the humble cardboard box! Pop out at the right time to catch unsuspecting foes completely off guard.

SILENCE IS GOLDEN

Most of the suppressed weapons were unvaulted this season. Most of these spy-friendly guns were typically found by raiding outposts.

SURPRISE RIDES

Most toilets and dumpsters allow you to hide inside, although some got a surprise when they jumped into one that carried them straight into an AI stronghold!

QUIZ: ARE YOU A FORTNITE EXPERT?

PROVE IT BY GUNNING FOR HIGH SCORES IN THIS TRICKY TRIVIA TEST

COMMON

THE EASY STUFF
(ONE point per correct answer)

1. How many players can take part in a standard Solo Battle Royale game?

2. Which of the following is NOT a building material in Fortnite: stone, paper, metal, or wood?

3. Name the shrinking barrier outside of the current safe zone.

UNCOMMON

PICKING UP THE PACE
(TWO points per correct answer)

4. Name the shady Outfit that was the Tier 100 Battle Pass reward in Chapter 2: Season 1.

5. How many different types of shotgun have been made available in Battle Royale?

← 6. This funky throwable item didn't do any damage. What effect did it have instead?

RARE

THE TRUE TEST BEGINS (THREE points per correct answer)

7. Which set features Outfits that show off the player's custom Banner emblem?

8. What is this Outfit called? ➡

9. Of all current and previous Battle Royale weapons, which can do the most damage with a single shot?

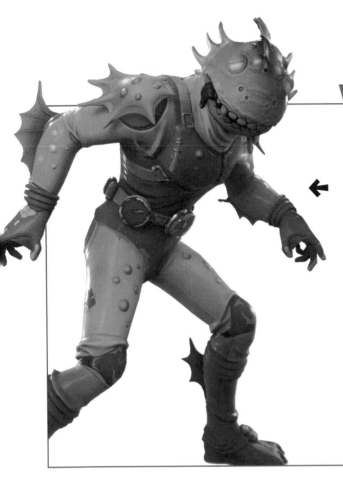

EXTRA SPICY! (FOUR points per correct answer)

← 10. In which season did this creepy Outfit make its debut?

[ ]

11. Name the two spy factions that take over the island in Chapter 2: Season 2.

[ ]

12. Can you name the first weapon to ever be Vaulted?

[ ]

LEGENDARY

GOOD LUCK...YOU'LL NEED IT! (FIVE points per correct answer)

13. In the history of the Battle Royale map up to Chapter 2: Season 2, only two named locations have ever had non-alliterative names. One is The Block, but what is the other?

[ ]

14. What is the name of this Glider?

[ ]

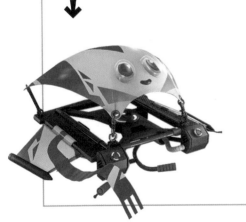

15. Two Outfits could be unlocked for purchase after sufficiently leveling up in Fortnite's very first season. Can you name them both? (five points for EACH correct answer—let's go out with a bang!)

[ ]

[ ]

HOW DID YOU DO?

Add up your points and let's see just how much you really know about Fortnite....

0-9
Somebody hasn't been paying attention. Try harder next time!

10-19
Get back on the Battle Bus—you still have a lot to learn.

20-29
Not bad at all. Some of those later ones were pretty tough, huh?

30-39
Pretty impressive—you clearly know your stuff!

40-49
So close to full marks, great work there.

50
A perfect score?! Nobody knows Fortnite as well as you!

Answers: 1. Paper, 3. The Storm, 4. Fusion, 5. Six: Combat, Double-Barrel, Drum, Heavy, Pump, and Tactical, 6. Anyone hit with a Boogie Bomb was forced to dance, 7. Banner Brigade, 8. Infinity, 9. Heavy Sniper Rifle (392 damage on a critical hit), 10. Season 4, 11. Ghost and Shadow, 12. The Zapotron, way back in Season 1, 13. Neo Tilted, during Season 9, 14. Flappy, 15. Aerial Assault Trooper and Renegade Raider

HEADLINE PUBLISHING GROUP
An Hachette UK Company
Carmelite House
50 Victoria Embankment
London, EC4 0DZ
www.headline.co.uk www.hachette.co.uk

Little, Brown and Company
Hachette Book Group
1290 Avenue of the Americas, New York, NY 10104
Visit us at hbgusa.com/Fortnite

www.epicgames.com